Solomon & Bernard

Chicago — Ill

July 1 – 1947

A PALESTINE PICTURE BOOK

A PALESTINE PICTURE BOOK

PHOTOGRAPHS BY JAKOB ROSNER

SCHOCKEN BOOKS / NEW YORK

MANUFACTURED IN THE UNITED STATES OF AMERICA

THE MURRAY PRINTING COMPANY
CAMBRIDGE, MASSACHUSETTS

PREFACE

Twenty-three miles wide in the north and eighty in the south, Palestine extends two hundred and forty miles along the Mediterranean. Rising 4,000 feet above sea level and dominated by the snow-clad peak of Mount Hermon, the hills of Galilee in the north enjoy a mild climate. To their south, the hot valley of Jezreel slopes gently eastward into the subtropic Jordan depression and Lake Chinnereth, far below sea level.

Farther to the south the coastal plain has a wider sweep. Fertile red-brown soil alternates with swamps and glaring desert sands, until the land rises a second time into the stony hills of Samaria. South of them, Jerusalem is built high on the peaks of Judea, its western suburbs overlooking the Mediterranean, its eastern limits stretching into the Judean desert, which drops steeply 3,800 feet into the Dead Sea. In the extreme south, the Negev, thousands of square miles of sun-scorched wasteland, is bordered by the Gulf of Aqaba and the desert of Sinai.

This is the land where man conceived the idea of one God, the land to which Jews, dispersed all over the world, have turned in prayer for two thousand years. Stony hills, water stagnating in the plains, the stifling heat of the Jordan valley, wadis parched dry in summer and overflowing with torrential streams during the short rainy winter months, shrubs buried under shifting desert sands, weeds and dust — these cover the remains of the civilization from which the faith and moral code of the West have emerged.

It is in this land that a unique constructive feat has been performed during a period when two world wars were laying waste the European continent. It is barely forty years since the large-scale Jewish colonization of Palestine was begun. Despite natural and political handicaps, Jewish colonization, once begun, continued — stubbornly. It changed the physiognomy of the land. It produced a new type of Jew. It re-created a Jewish Palestine.

Cities have sprung up on sites which were barren sand and rock a generation ago. Hundreds of agricultural settlements and villages have been built; swamps have been drained and desert soil irrigated.

Palestine has seen the successful development of a new form of co-operative society in the many rural settlements where the land belongs to the nation and all property is shared in common. It has witnessed the immigration of hundreds of thousands of European Jews, as well as the return of many of the Oriental Jewish communities.

Jakob Rosner, the photographer, is intimately acquainted with Palestine through his years of work for the Jewish National Fund. He has deliberately avoided the controversial issues that at times tend to overshadow, in the eyes of the outside world, the patient and inspired labor that goes forward daily in Jewish Palestine. He has sought rather to record the large achievements of this patience and this labor.

TABLE OF CONTENTS

I

THE LAND

Palestine—about twenty-three miles wide in the north and eighty miles wide in the south—stretches for two hundred and forty miles along the Mediterranean.

The Mediterranean Coast near Pituah

In the north the coastal plain sweeps quickly to the foothills.

Inland from the port of Haifa, in the direction of Mount Gilboa, lies the Valley of Jezreel (or Esdraelon), now known as the "Emek."

Long a barren waste, it has been transformed by Jewish settlers into a place of fertile fields and green gardens in a generation's time.

14

A Jewish farmer's sheep water at the Spring of Harod, where in the time of the Judges Gideon tested his soldiers.

Forests planted by the Jewish National Fund (Keren Kayemeth Leisrael) restore the treeless land to its original condition of beauty and fertility.

Balfour Forest

In the north, where Galilee stretches from the Syrian border to the Emek, rich and diversified crops wait to be harvested.

Orange plantations now cover thousands of acres of the once water-starved coastal plain . . .

Near Even Yehudah

. . . in dramatic contrast with the parched tracts of soil where colonization has not yet begun.

Between Mount Carmel and the Mountains of Ephraim

Palestine is rich in scenic change. Near the northern border, flat, grassy meadows lie close against gracefully sloping hills.

Wide, mountainous vistas are disclosed as one ascends from the coastal plain into the mountains of Ephraim.

Buried beneath these dunes is the ancient city of Caesarea, the port of Herod the Great, a prey to the shifting sands . . .

. . . that the modern settler must continually combat in order to preserve his trees and fields.

Near Tel Aviv

In winter, after the rains, torrential streams race through these gorges; in summer, the oleander blooms in the dry beds.

Wadi Amud

Pinewoods on Mount Carmel are the imposing remnants of the forests that covered
large parts of Palestine in biblical times.

Past and present blend everywhere in Palestine. This is the entrance to the Cata-
combs of Beth Shearim, site of the Sanhedrin in the second century C.E. Rabbi Judah
ha-Nasi, the compiler of the Mishnah, is buried here.

The Arbel, in whose fortified caves the Maccabees sheltered, towers high upon a plateau near Lake Chinnereth.

Giant millstones, relics of an ancient system of agriculture, lie scattered on the ground.

Capernaum

The massive horizontal pillars of the ancient Mediterranean port of Caesarea testify to the great scale on which the city was built.

The ruins of this fourth-century synagogue at Capernaum, an outstanding example of Jewish architecture, have recently been excavated and partially restored.

II

THE JORDAN

II

High in the north, in the region of Mount Hermon, the Jordan has its source in several springs, one of which, near the site of the biblical city of Dan, is known as Ain-ed-Dan.

At first a tiny stream . . .

. . . it unites with other streams to form the River Jordan, and flows southward over small falls . . .

. . . and through swamps of reed and papyrus into Lake Huleh, the biblical "Waters of Merom."

Leaving Lake Huleh, the Jordan begins to fall below sea level . . .

. . . and makes a precipitous descent past the gloomy bastion of the Arbel . . .

. . into Lake Chinnereth . . .

. . . also called the Sea of Tiberias, the Sea of Galilee, and the Lake of Gennesaret.

On its western shore is the city of Tiberias, which Joseph ha-Nasi, Duke of Naxos, rebuilt in the sixteenth century above the ruins of the ancient city with the intention of inviting Jewish colonists all over the world to settle there.

Its old city wall reaches out into the lake.

High above Tiberias is the newly developed suburb of Kiryat Shmuel.

The tomb of Rabbi Meir Baal ha-Nes, reputedly the Rabbi Meir of the Mishnaic period, and the synagogues erected above it lie to the south of Tiberias . . .

. . . near the hot springs in whose medicinal waters people have bathed for more than
two thousand years, and where modern baths are now being constructed.

From Lake Chinnereth the Jordan flows through a wide valley studded with new and thriving Jewish settlements . . .

. . . past the mound of Beth-Shan, once a center of Canaanite civilization, in Hellenistic times the site of the city of Scythopolis, and through the ages a fortress that has dominated the vital route from Egypt to the territories east of the Jordan.

The hydro-electric resources of the Jordan, thanks to the initiative of Pinhas Rutenberg, are now being exploited. Sluice gates . . .

. . . and dams, erected along the Jordan and its tributary, the Yarmuk, convert water power into electricity.

The Jordan sweeps past Kfar Ruppin, southernmost settlement in the Jordan valley . . .

. . . passes into subtropical country, where dense vegetation covers its steep, stratified banks . . .

. . . until, at the end of its course, 1300 feet below sea level, it empties into the Dead Sea.

III

TWO CITIES

Haifa, situated at the foot of Mount Carmel, is Palestine's chief seaport.

Its harbor was constructed between 1929 and 1933 and has greatly facilitated the growth of industry.

The city is constantly expanding, and today large numbers of workers live in developments built along the farther reaches of Haifa Bay on ground purchased by the Jewish National Fund.

Tel Aviv. In twenty-five years its all-Jewish population has reached a figure of more
than 200,000.

During the war Jewish volunteers from all over the country marched down Allenby
Road to join the Allied armies.

A steady stream of traffic passes along its wide avenues . . .

Allenby Road

. . . and a fleet of modern busses provides transportation to any part of Tel Aviv and Palestine.

Tel Aviv's beaches, where lifeguards keep a careful watch, are part of an elaborate municipal recreational plan . . .

. . . as are the promenades and shore drives . . .

. . . the tree-lined avenues . . .

Rothschild Boulevard

. . . and the parks and playgrounds, where the city's population enjoys its Sabbath rest.

The workers' sections, built to provide for the health, convenience, and welfare of their inhabitants, are models of advanced urban design.

Sterot Nordau

Outside Tel Aviv is Kiryat Avodah, a workers' suburb . . .

. . . where, within easy reach of the city, some of the pleasures of the country can be had.

IV

RURAL SETTLEMENT

Ever since 1908, when organized Zionist agricultural resettlement began with the establishment of Deganiah in the Jordan valley, the youth have been the pioneers of the movement. Living in tents . . .

Nes Tsionah

. . . or little, mushroom-shaped houses, they have devoted their life and labor to the one aim of developing their settlements into strong and efficient units.

Maayon (Zichron Yaakov)

Many of the new agricultural colonies are either of the type *kvutzot*, or *kibbutzim* — collective settlements founded and financed by the Palestine Foundation Fund (Keren Hayesod), and established on nationally owned land.

At the Foot of Mount Gilboa

The first buildings, which are generally temporary structures built of wood ..

Hulata

. . . are gradually replaced, according to a careful plan, by the stone houses . . .

. . . silos, playgrounds, and landscaped prospects of the permanent settlement.

Tel Yosef

Dafneh, a northern settlement in Upper Galilee, was founded in 1939. The signal tower, of vital importance in communication and defense, was erected first, in one night; houses and farm buildings were then constructed around it.

Revivim, south of Beersheba, is so far only an experimental station for the investigation of the climatic and agricultural conditions of the Negev, the southern part of Palestine.

All collective settlements . . .

Tel Amal

. . . have community kitchens and dining halls for the adults.

Merhaviah

The fully developed settlements are often equipped with modern electric household appliances.

Both the collective settlements and the Mosheve Ovedim (co-operative settlements of smallholders who do not own the land they work but hold it under a hereditary lease from the Jewish National Fund) are principally engaged in the cultivation of the soil...

Givat Hashloshah

. . . and stock and dairy farming, under the guidance of instructors, and helped by the continual work of the agricultural research stations.

Some settlements, to supplement their income, take up a specialized activity like beekeeping.

Gan Shmuel

Others, especially settlements located in the Jordan Valley and the low regions of the Emek, have developed fisheries.

A number of settlements have founded industries directly to exploit their agricultural products. Givat Brenner, for example, has a marmalade cannery . . .

. . . that possesses modern machinery and is scientifically operated.

Givat Brenner

These achievements have not been the work of one generation. This farmer came to Palestine with the second Aliyah, during the immigration period of 1905–1914, worked long hours as a hired laborer, and then in 1922 became one of the founders of Kfar Yehezkel, a co-operative settlement established by the Palestine Foundation Fund.

Kfar Yehezkel

His son, brought up on the settlement, now shoulders the main responsibilities of house and land . . .

. . . and the third generation prepares itself . . .

. . . to carry on the work of their fathers and grandfathers.

The Youth Aliyah brought to Palestine young and enthusiastic European immigrants who had been previously prepared in training camps and were eager to merge with the old Yishuv.

Kfar Yehezkel

Older people, some of them fathers and mothers of the young settlers, left Europe
to join the settlements, and now contribute their share to the labor of the group.

Tel Yosef

But the pioneering work is not yet finished. Day after day, incessantly and inspiredly, it is carried forward by such people as this Jerusalem-born youth . . .

Hafets Hayim

. . . and this plowman of the rocky slopes of Kfar Etsion.

The children are given careful study and attention. When a settlement is founded, the communal children's house — where the boys and girls live — is among the first to be erected. Nurseries . . .

Bet Oren

. . . and kindergartens, supervised by trained nurses, are found in every settlement.

Ain Hashofet

The children learn arts . . .

Givat Brenner

. . . and crafts.

Kfar Yehezkel

The schoolhouses are large and recreational facilities ample.

Givat Brenner

Agricultural training begins at an early age. Children live and work in a school community that reproduces the work of the settlement in all its details.

Mishmar Ha-Emek

After graduation most city children regard it their duty to spend a year working on a farm.

Merhaviah

Agricultural schools complete the theoretical and practical training of the Palestinian farmer.

Refugee children are given special instruction to prepare them . . .

Bet Oren

. . . for a new life.

The harvest festival is the climax of the year, when, to the sound of flutes . . .

Avihayil

. . . and the rattle of tambourines, Zion's past is linked to the present hopes of the settlers for the success of their labor.

Daliah

It is for such success that this minyan of nine farmers and one watchman, gathered together for the afternoon prayers, beseeches God: 'Bless this year unto us, together with every kind of the produce thereof, for our welfare; give a blessing upon the face of the earth.'

Kfar Etsion

V

INTERLUDE:
THE YEMENITE JEWS IN PALESTINE

In 1882 the first group of Yemenite Jews arrived in Palestine. In the past forty years more have managed to leave the remote and isolated regions of Arabian Yemen, and today their number in Palestine is considerably larger. In the cities, many of the Yemenite Jews pursue their traditional crafts, usually gold- and silversmithing.

Jerusalem

Some of the recent immigrants, however, finding it difficult to adjust to modern conditions, are obliged to be the porters . . .

. . . laundresses, and housemaids of the city.

Tel Aviv

Yemenite Jews are a strongly traditional element of Palestinian Jewry. In rural environments they steadfastly maintain their ancient Oriental way of life . . .

Kfar Shiloah

. . . and even in the cities the Yemenites are reluctant to abandon their age-old techniques, such as the primitive hand mill that this recent immigrant brought from Arabia.

Marmorek-Rehovot

This hood has been part of the holiday dress of Yemenite women for centuries.

Tel Aviv

Men and women smoke the narghile . . .

Kfar Shiloah

. . . often a precious family heirloom.

Near Rishon le-Zion

The respect in which they hold learning . . .

. . . and scholarship is traditional.

Marmorek-Rehovot

The art of the scribe still flourishes.

Daily, the men gather in the synagogue and house of study (called the *knis*).

On the eve of the Sabbath, dressed in their holiday white silk, they are deep in study.

On Saturday afternoon the family listens to the reading of the Psalms.

Kfar Shiloah

Despite the Yemenites' veneration of the learned man, in most instances the old-fashioned heder represents the only schooling a boy receives.

Marmorek-Rehovot

Efforts are being made to raise the educational and economic level of the Yemenites. Progressive schools emphasizing the traditional skills of the Yemenite Jews are preparing the youth to take its place in modern Palestine.

Maya Rosenberg School, Rehovot

VI

JERUSALEM

The Jerusalem road mounts upward through the Valley of Kidron, past the Tomb
of Absalom . . .

. . . between an old Jewish burial ground and the wall of the Old City, into Jerusalem.

Many centuries have contributed to the growth of the city. This section of the wall, at the southeast corner of the Temple area, dates from the time of Herod.

Visible across the roofs of the Old City is the Mosque of Omar, built on the site of Solomon's Temple.

At the western side of the Temple area stands the Wailing Wall, the sole surviving remnant of Herod's Temple.

About 1860, Jews began to build outside the Old City. The modern residential sections of the New City, with their wide streets and open parks, are in striking contrast with the old Jerusalem.

Here Jewish children grow to maturity, playful, curious, and open-eyed.

Even in modern Jerusalem the colorful Jewish tradition lives on — in this colony of Bokharan Jews, for example, who come from the Russo-Persian border and continue their time-honored way of life in their synagogues . . .

. . . and homes — which, like this *sukkah*, are brightly carpeted and hung with old and precious tapestries.

The Rothschild-Hadassah-University Hospital and the Postgraduate Medical School ...

. . . constitute the largest medical center in the Near East.

On Mount Scopus, overlooking old and new Jerusalem, is the Hebrew University, a seat of Jewish learning and general research.

The constant growth of the University enables it to play a greater and greater role in the advancement of science and a new Jewish way of life.

Photographs on pages 11 to 137, by Jakob Rosner, Tel Aviv
Photographs on pages 138 to 141, by Alfred Bernheim, Jerusalem

The constant growth of the University enables it to play a greater and greater role
in the advancement of science and a new Jewish way of life.

Photographs on pages 11 to 137, by Jakob Rosner, Tel Aviv
Photographs on pages 138 to 141, by Alfred Bernheim, Jerusalem